Navigating Bipolar 1: A Comprehensive Guide to Managing Your Symptoms

Welcome to Your Journey

Welcome to "Navigating Bipolar 1: A Comprehensive Guide to Managing Your Symptoms." This journey is about empowerment, understanding, and reclaiming control over your life. You are not alone in facing bipolar 1 disorder, and this book is your companion on the path to stability.

Breaking Down the Stigma: Understanding Bipolar 1

Let's begin by dismantling the stigma surrounding bipolar 1. It's crucial to recognize that bipolar 1 is not a character flaw or a weakness. It is a medical condition, just like any other, and you deserve compassion and understanding. By understanding the science behind bipolar 1, you can better navigate its challenges.

Bipolar 1 involves manic and depressive episodes, each presenting unique struggles. The unpredictability of these episodes can be daunting, but through knowledge and self-awareness, you can learn to anticipate and manage them effectively.

Motivation Quote: "Your journey with bipolar 1 is a testament to your strength. Embrace it, learn from it, and grow through it."

The Importance of Seeking Professional Help

Seeking professional help is a crucial step in your journey to stability. A mental health professional can provide an accurate diagnosis, personalized treatment plan, and ongoing support. This chapter emphasizes the importance of reaching out to a psychiatrist, therapist, or counselor who specializes in mood disorders.

Professional guidance is not a sign of weakness but a courageous step towards a healthier future. Together, we'll explore the diagnostic process, helping you navigate the emotions that come with it.

Self-Esteem Boost: "Taking the first step towards seeking help is an act of self-love. You are deserving of support, understanding, and a life filled with stability."

As you embark on this journey, remember that knowledge is power. Understanding bipolar 1 and seeking professional help are the foundation stones for building a life of stability and fulfillment. In the next chapter, we'll dive deeper into the nuances of bipolar 1 disorder and how it manifests in your life.

Chapter 1: Decoding Bipolar 1 Disorder

What is Bipolar 1? A Closer Look at the Disorder

Welcome to the heart of understanding bipolar 1 disorder. In this chapter, we'll unravel the intricacies of this condition, providing you with insights that empower you to navigate its challenges.

Bipolar 1 Defined: Bipolar 1 disorder is a mental health condition characterized by extreme mood swings. These swings consist of manic episodes, where individuals experience heightened energy, euphoria, and sometimes erratic behavior, and depressive episodes, marked by overwhelming sadness and a lack of interest or pleasure in activities.

Understanding the nature of these episodes is fundamental to managing bipolar 1. Manic episodes are not just bursts of energy; they can lead to impulsive decisions and risky behaviors. Depressive episodes, on the other hand, can be paralyzing, affecting daily functioning and overall well-being.

Your Unique Experience: It's essential to recognize that bipolar 1 manifests uniquely in each individual. Your experience may differ from others, and that's perfectly normal. By understanding the broad spectrum of symptoms and their potential variations, you gain a clearer picture of your own journey.

Motivation Quote: "In embracing your uniqueness, you unlock the door to your personal strength. Your journey with bipolar 1 is one of resilience and growth."

Recognizing the Spectrum: Understanding Manic and Depressive Episodes

Bipolar 1 disorder operates on a spectrum, and within this spectrum lie the distinct characteristics of manic and depressive episodes.

Manic Episodes: During manic episodes, you may feel a surge of energy, creativity, and an intense euphoria. However, this heightened state can lead to impulsive decision-making, risk-taking, and challenges in maintaining focus. Recognizing the signs of a manic episode is crucial for implementing strategies to manage and stabilize your mood.

Depressive Episodes: Depressive episodes bring about profound sadness, fatigue, and a sense of hopelessness. Daily tasks may become overwhelming, and the world may lose its color. Identifying the early signs of a depressive episode allows for proactive intervention and support.

Balancing Act: The Mixed Episode: In some instances, bipolar 1 may present mixed episodes, where features of both manic and depressive states coexist. Understanding this delicate balance is essential for tailoring coping mechanisms that address the complexities of mixed episodes.

The Role of Genetics and Environmental Factors

Bipolar 1 disorder often involves a combination of genetic and environmental factors.

Genetic Predisposition: Research indicates a genetic component in bipolar disorders. If you have a family history of bipolar or related conditions, it may increase your risk. However, genetics alone don't determine your destiny; environmental factors play a significant role.

Environmental Triggers: Stressful life events, trauma, and disruptions in circadian rhythms can trigger episodes. By identifying and managing these triggers, you gain more control over your condition.

Self-Esteem Boost: "Your journey with bipolar 1 is not a predetermined path but a canvas of possibilities. You have the strength to shape and color your narrative."

Understanding bipolar 1 disorder is a journey in self-discovery. As we move forward, we'll delve into the diagnostic process, helping you navigate this path with resilience and optimism. Remember, knowledge is your ally in this voyage towards stability.

Chapter 2: The Diagnostic Journey

Seeking Professional Diagnosis: The First Step to Understanding

Embarking on the diagnostic journey is a significant stride towards understanding and managing bipolar 1 disorder. This chapter focuses on the importance of seeking professional help, guiding you through the process and preparing you for the insights that lie ahead.

Taking the Initiative: Recognizing the signs and symptoms of bipolar 1 in yourself is a commendable first step. However, a formal diagnosis from a mental health professional is crucial for tailored treatment. This journey starts with your decision to seek help, an empowering choice that sets the stage for understanding and managing your condition.

The Role of a Mental Health Professional: Psychiatrists, psychologists, or clinical counselors experienced in mood disorders play a vital role in the diagnostic process. They conduct comprehensive assessments, considering your symptoms, medical history, and overall well-being. Your honesty and openness during this process pave the way for accurate diagnosis and effective treatment planning.

Motivation Quote: "Seeking help is not a sign of weakness; it's a testament to your courage and commitment to a healthier, more stable future."

Interpreting Psychiatric Evaluations and Assessments

The diagnostic journey involves various evaluations and assessments designed to unveil the nuances of bipolar 1 disorder.

Clinical Interviews: A mental health professional conducts detailed interviews to gather information about your experiences, emotions, and behaviors. Sharing your thoughts openly provides valuable insights into your mental health.

Questionnaires and Rating Scales: Standardized assessments may be employed to quantify the severity of symptoms and monitor changes over time. These tools contribute to a more comprehensive understanding of your condition.

Observations and Behavioral Analysis: Your actions and reactions in various situations offer additional clues. Behavioral analysis helps to identify patterns and triggers, aiding in a more accurate diagnosis.

Navigating the Emotional Impact of Diagnosis

Receiving a bipolar 1 diagnosis can evoke a range of emotions – relief, validation, fear, or even uncertainty. It's crucial to acknowledge and navigate these emotions constructively.

Validation and Relief: For many, a formal diagnosis provides validation for their experiences. It becomes a crucial step towards understanding the challenges faced and opens the door to targeted interventions and support.

Fear and Uncertainty: On the flip side, the diagnosis may instill fear or uncertainty about the future. It's essential to remember that a diagnosis is not a life sentence; rather, it's a tool for crafting an informed and effective approach to managing bipolar 1.

Self-Esteem Boost: "Acknowledging your emotions is a strength, not a vulnerability. You have the resilience to face and overcome the challenges that lie ahead."

As we delve deeper into your journey, remember that the diagnostic process is a significant milestone. Understanding your condition lays the foundation for a personalized and effective treatment plan. In the upcoming chapter, we'll explore the various treatment options available and how they contribute to your path of stability.

Chapter 3: Medication Management and Treatment Options

Medications for Stabilization: An Overview

Understanding the role of medications in managing bipolar 1 disorder is crucial for achieving stability. In this chapter, we'll explore the various medications commonly prescribed and their impact on stabilizing mood.

Mood Stabilizers: Medications like lithium, valproate, and carbamazepine are often prescribed to stabilize mood swings. They work by regulating neurotransmitters and preventing extreme highs and lows. It's essential to discuss potential side effects and regularly monitor blood levels to ensure their efficacy.

Antipsychotics: In some cases, antipsychotic medications like olanzapine or risperidone may be recommended to manage manic episodes. These medications help control erratic behavior and restore balance to your mood.

Antidepressants: For depressive episodes, selective serotonin reuptake inhibitors (SSRIs) or other antidepressants may be prescribed. However, their use is often cautious, as they can trigger manic episodes in some individuals.

Motivation Quote: "Medications are tools in your toolkit, not a definition of who you are. They help sculpt the path, but it's your strength that paves the way."

Balancing Act: Finding the Right Medication

Achieving the right balance with medications is a collaborative process between you and your healthcare provider.

Individualized Treatment Plans: Every person responds differently to medications. Your healthcare provider will work closely with you to tailor a treatment plan that addresses your specific symptoms and minimizes side effects.

Communication is Key: Open communication about your experiences, side effects, and concerns is vital. If a medication doesn't feel right or causes intolerable side effects, don't hesitate to discuss it with your provider. Finding the right balance often involves some trial and error.

Regular Monitoring: Medication effectiveness can change over time, and your dosage may need adjustments. Regular check-ins with your healthcare provider ensure that your treatment plan evolves with your needs.

Complementary Therapies: Exploring Adjunct Treatments

Beyond medications, complementary therapies play a significant role in managing bipolar 1 disorder.

Therapy and Counseling: Individual or group therapy provides a supportive space to explore emotions, develop coping strategies, and enhance self-awareness.

Cognitive-behavioral therapy (CBT) is particularly effective in addressing thought patterns associated with bipolar 1.

Mindfulness and Meditation: Practices like mindfulness and meditation contribute to overall well-being. They help manage stress, improve focus, and enhance emotional regulation, providing valuable tools for navigating the challenges of bipolar 1.

Lifestyle Modifications: Healthy lifestyle choices, including regular exercise, a balanced diet, and sufficient sleep, complement medication and therapy. These modifications contribute to the overall stability of your mood.

Self-Esteem Boost: "Your commitment to exploring various treatment options showcases your dedication to personal well-being. You are actively sculpting a life of stability and fulfillment."

As you consider medication management and treatment options, remember that this journey is uniquely yours. The collaboration between you and your healthcare team is a powerful force in achieving and maintaining stability. In the next chapter, we'll delve into the importance of building a robust support system to enhance your resilience and overall well-being.

Chapter 4: Building a Support System

The Power of Connection: Sharing Your Diagnosis

Navigating bipolar 1 disorder is not a solitary journey. Building a robust support system is essential for resilience and overall well-being. In this chapter, we'll explore the transformative power of connection, starting with sharing your diagnosis.

Breaking the Silence: Opening up about your bipolar 1 diagnosis can be both liberating and challenging. It's a personal decision, but sharing your experiences with trusted individuals can foster understanding and empathy. Begin with those closest to you, who can provide support as you navigate the complexities of the disorder.

Educating Others: Sharing educational resources about bipolar 1 can aid in dispelling myths and fostering a more accurate understanding. Providing information about the disorder equips your support system with the knowledge needed to offer meaningful assistance.

Motivation Quote: "In vulnerability, there is strength. Sharing your journey is not a sign of weakness but a testament to your courage."

Educating Friends and Family: Creating a Supportive Network

Your friends and family play a pivotal role in your support system. Educating them about bipolar 1 helps create an environment of understanding and compassion.

Open Communication: Encourage open dialogue about bipolar 1 within your family and friend circle. Discussing your experiences, triggers, and coping mechanisms creates a supportive atmosphere where everyone can contribute positively.

Setting Boundaries: Establishing clear boundaries ensures that your support system respects your needs. Communicate what support looks like for you during different phases of the disorder, promoting a collaborative and harmonious relationship.

Family Therapy: Engaging in family therapy sessions can provide a structured space for communication and understanding. A therapist can guide discussions, address concerns, and facilitate healthy interactions within the family unit.

Peer Support Groups: Finding Understanding Beyond Loved Ones

While the support of friends and family is invaluable, connecting with peers who share similar experiences offers a unique form of understanding.

Joining Supportive Communities: Peer support groups bring together individuals facing similar challenges. These communities provide a safe space to share, learn, and connect with others who truly understand the nuances of living with bipolar 1.

Online Communities and Forums: Virtual spaces allow for connection with a broader community. Engaging in online forums or social media groups can provide a sense of belonging and immediate support, especially during challenging times.

Self-Esteem Boost: "Building a support system is an affirmation of your worthiness. You deserve understanding, empathy, and a network that uplifts you."

As you cultivate your support system, remember that vulnerability is a strength, and seeking support is an act of self-love. In the next chapter, we'll explore the importance of lifestyle modifications in enhancing stability and overall well-being.

Chapter 5: Lifestyle Modifications for Stability

The Impact of Sleep on Bipolar 1: Establishing Healthy Routines

Creating a stable and nurturing lifestyle is fundamental to managing bipolar 1 disorder. In this chapter, we'll delve into the profound impact of sleep on mood stability and explore strategies to establish healthy routines.

The Sleep-Mood Connection: Sleep plays a crucial role in regulating mood, and disruptions can trigger manic or depressive episodes. Establishing a consistent sleep routine, including a set bedtime and wake-up time, contributes to mood stability.

Creating a Sleep-Optimized Environment: Transform your sleep space into a haven for rest. Dim the lights before bedtime, keep the room cool, and minimize screen time to promote a conducive environment for quality sleep.

Recognizing Sleep Patterns: Monitor your sleep patterns and identify any correlations with mood shifts. This awareness allows for proactive adjustments in your routine to maintain stability.

Motivation Quote: "In the rhythm of a good night's sleep, you find the harmony for a stable and fulfilling day. Prioritize your rest as an essential pillar of your well-being."

Nutrition and Exercise: Supporting Mental Health

A balanced diet and regular exercise contribute significantly to mental health and overall well-being.

Nutritional Considerations: Certain dietary choices can impact mood. Explore a diet rich in whole foods, incorporating fruits, vegetables, lean proteins, and omega-3 fatty acids. Limiting caffeine and sugar intake can also contribute to stability.

Exercise for Mood Regulation: Physical activity has profound effects on mental health. Regular exercise releases endorphins, reduces stress, and contributes to better sleep. Find activities you enjoy, whether it's walking, dancing, or yoga, and make them a part of your routine.

Mindful Eating Practices: Practice mindful eating to foster a healthy relationship with food. Pay attention to hunger and fullness cues, savor each bite, and cultivate a positive connection with nourishment.

Stress Management Techniques

Stress is a common trigger for bipolar 1 episodes. Developing effective stress management techniques is essential for maintaining stability.

Mindfulness and Meditation: Incorporate mindfulness and meditation into your daily routine. These practices help ground you in the present moment, reduce anxiety, and enhance overall emotional well-being.

Breathing Exercises: Simple breathing exercises can be powerful tools for stress management. Practice deep, intentional breathing during moments of tension to calm the nervous system.

Establishing Boundaries: Recognize your limits and communicate effectively to establish boundaries in your personal and professional life. Saying no when needed and prioritizing self-care contribute to stress reduction.

Self-Esteem Boost: "In nourishing your body and mind, you cultivate the strength to face life's challenges. Each nutritious meal and mindful breath is a step towards your well-being."

As you integrate lifestyle modifications into your routine, remember that small, consistent changes yield significant results. In the next chapter, we'll explore strategies for recognizing triggers and early warning signs, empowering you to navigate your journey with greater self-awareness and resilience.

Chapter 6: Understanding Triggers and Early Warning Signs

Identifying Personal Triggers: A Reflective Exercise

Understanding your personal triggers is a pivotal step in managing bipolar 1 disorder. In this chapter, we'll embark on a reflective exercise to help identify the factors that may contribute to episodes.

Self-Reflection: Take a moment to reflect on past episodes and note the circumstances surrounding them. Consider stressors, changes in routine, or specific situations that preceded mood shifts. This self-awareness lays the groundwork for recognizing and addressing potential triggers.

Journaling: Maintain a journal to track your emotions, daily activities, and any significant events. Over time, patterns may emerge, offering valuable insights into your unique triggers. Regular journaling enhances self-awareness and aids in proactive management.

Seeking Input from Others: Engage in open communication with your support system. Loved ones and friends may provide perspectives on your behavior and identify patterns that you might overlook.

Motivation Quote: "In understanding your triggers, you wield the power to navigate your journey with intention. Your awareness is the compass guiding you to stability."

Recognizing Early Warning Signs of Episodes

Early detection of mood shifts is instrumental in implementing timely interventions. This chapter explores the nuanced signs that may herald an impending episode.

Emotional Changes: Pay attention to shifts in your emotional landscape. Increased irritability, persistent sadness, or heightened anxiety may signal the onset of an episode.

Cognitive Patterns: Notice changes in your thought patterns. Racing thoughts, difficulty concentrating, or a surge in creativity that feels uncontrollable may indicate a shift in mood.

Physical Symptoms: Changes in sleep patterns, energy levels, or appetite can serve as early indicators. Physical symptoms often accompany shifts in mood and can offer valuable clues.

Developing a Crisis Plan for Effective Coping

Preparation is key in managing crises effectively. Develop a crisis plan to navigate challenging moments with a structured and proactive approach.

Identifying Support Contacts: Compile a list of trusted contacts you can reach out to during a crisis. This may include friends, family members, or mental health professionals. Share your crisis plan with them to ensure a coordinated response.

Coping Strategies: Outline coping strategies that have proven effective for you in the past. Whether it's engaging in creative outlets, practicing mindfulness, or seeking professional support, having a toolkit of coping mechanisms enhances your resilience.

Emergency Resources: Include emergency contact information for mental health hotlines or crisis intervention services in your plan. Having readily accessible resources ensures immediate assistance when needed.

Self-Esteem Boost: "Developing a crisis plan is an act of self-empowerment. You possess the strength to face challenges head-on and navigate your journey with resilience."

As you delve into the intricacies of recognizing triggers and early warning signs, remember that self-awareness is a continual process. In the next chapter, we'll explore coping strategies specifically tailored for depressive episodes, empowering you to navigate these challenging moments with strength and purpose.

Chapter 7: Coping Strategies for Depressive Episodes

Cognitive Behavioral Techniques for Managing Depressive Thoughts

Coping with depressive episodes involves navigating the labyrinth of negative thoughts and emotions. This chapter introduces cognitive-behavioral techniques to empower you in managing depressive thoughts.

Identifying Negative Thought Patterns: Begin by recognizing negative thought patterns that contribute to depressive feelings. Common distortions include black-and-white thinking, catastrophizing, and self-blame. Understanding these patterns is the first step towards changing them.

Challenging Negative Thoughts: Actively challenge negative thoughts by questioning their validity. Ask yourself if there's evidence supporting these thoughts or if they represent an exaggerated perspective. Developing a habit of challenging and reframing negative thoughts promotes a more balanced mindset.

Behavioral Activation: Engage in activities that bring a sense of accomplishment and joy, even when motivation is low. Behavioral activation involves breaking down tasks into smaller, manageable steps, gradually reintroducing structure and purpose into your routine.

Motivation Quote: "In challenging your thoughts, you reclaim control over your narrative. Each positive affirmation is a step towards the light."

Incorporating Mindfulness and Meditation

Mindfulness and meditation are powerful tools for navigating the depths of depressive episodes, fostering a sense of presence and inner peace.

Mindfulness Practices: Practice mindfulness by bringing attention to the present moment. Mindful breathing, body scans, or guided meditations can help ground you and alleviate the overwhelming nature of depressive thoughts.

Cultivating a Meditation Routine: Incorporate meditation into your daily routine. Start with short sessions and gradually increase the duration. Meditation cultivates self-awareness, enhances emotional regulation, and provides a sanctuary of calm during turbulent times.

Mindful Self-Compassion: Extend compassion towards yourself during depressive episodes. Treat yourself with the same kindness you would offer a friend facing similar challenges. Mindful self-compassion is a transformative practice in cultivating resilience.

Seeking Professional Help During Depressive Episodes

During depressive episodes, seeking professional help is a crucial step towards understanding and managing your condition effectively.

Therapeutic Support: Engage in therapy sessions, such as cognitive-behavioral therapy (CBT) or psychodynamic therapy, tailored to address depressive symptoms. Therapists provide a supportive space for exploring underlying issues and developing coping strategies.

Medication Adjustment: If you're on medication, consult with your psychiatrist about potential adjustments during depressive episodes. Fine-tuning your medication plan in collaboration with a healthcare professional ensures a holistic approach to managing symptoms.

Emergency Support: Know when to reach out for emergency support. If depressive thoughts become overwhelming, contact your mental health professional, a crisis hotline, or go to the nearest emergency room for immediate assistance.

Self-Esteem Boost: "Seeking professional help is a courageous act of self-love. You are deserving of support, and reaching out is a testament to your resilience."

As you incorporate these coping strategies into your toolkit, remember that depressive episodes are temporary. In the next chapter, we'll explore strategies for managing manic episodes and maintaining stability during periods of heightened energy and activity.

Chapter 8: Riding the Manic Wave: Strategies for Stability

Channeling Energy Productively: Creative Outlets

Navigating manic episodes involves channeling heightened energy into productive and positive outlets. This chapter explores creative avenues to harness your energy constructively.

Creative Expression: Engage in artistic pursuits such as painting, writing, or music. Creative expression provides an outlet for the surplus energy associated with manic episodes while fostering a sense of accomplishment.

Physical Activities: Participate in high-energy physical activities, like dance or sports. Channeling excess energy into movement not only benefits your physical well-being but also helps regulate mood during manic phases.

Mindful Creativity: Combine creativity with mindfulness practices. Explore activities like mindful coloring or crafting, where you can immerse yourself in the present moment while channeling your creative energy.

Motivation Quote: "Your creativity is a powerful force. In channeling your energy, you not only express yourself but also cultivate stability."

Establishing Routine During Manic Phases

Creating a structured routine is essential for managing manic episodes. Establishing a sense of order helps regulate your energy and maintain stability.

Daily Schedule: Develop a daily schedule that includes set times for activities such as meals, work, exercise, and relaxation. Consistency in routine provides a sense of predictability during periods of heightened energy.

Prioritizing Sleep: Maintain a consistent sleep routine, even during manic phases. Prioritize quality sleep by creating a calming bedtime routine and avoiding stimulants before bedtime.

Time Management: Break down tasks into manageable segments to prevent becoming overwhelmed. Effective time management contributes to a sense of accomplishment without risking burnout.

Medication Adherence: A Key to Manic Episode Management

Adhering to your medication plan is crucial for managing manic episodes effectively. This chapter emphasizes the importance of medication in stabilizing mood during periods of heightened activity.

Consistent Medication Schedule: Follow a consistent medication schedule as prescribed by your healthcare provider. Consistency is vital for maintaining therapeutic levels of medication in your system.

Open Communication with Healthcare Provider: Regularly communicate with your healthcare provider about any changes in symptoms or side effects. Adjustments to your medication plan may be necessary during manic phases.

Education and Awareness: Stay informed about your medications. Understanding how they work and their potential side effects enhances your ability to manage your condition proactively.

Self-Esteem Boost: "Your commitment to stability through medication adherence is an affirmation of your strength and resilience. You are actively shaping your path to wellness."

As you explore these strategies for managing manic episodes, remember that stability is achievable. In the next chapter, we'll delve into the dynamics of relationships and communication, providing insights into nurturing healthy connections during different phases of bipolar 1 disorder.

Chapter 9: Relationships and Communication

Nurturing Healthy Relationships: Communication Tips

Maintaining healthy relationships while navigating bipolar 1 involves effective communication and mutual understanding. This chapter explores communication tips to foster strong and supportive connections.

Open and Honest Dialogue: Encourage open communication with your loved ones. Share your thoughts and feelings, and create a space where they feel comfortable expressing their concerns. Honest dialogue is the foundation of a healthy relationship.

Active Listening: Practice active listening to truly understand your loved ones' perspectives. Validate their feelings and respond with empathy. This fosters a sense of mutual respect and strengthens your connection.

Expressing Gratitude: Regularly express gratitude for the support you receive. Acknowledge the efforts your loved ones make to understand and be there for you. Gratitude reinforces positive communication and builds a supportive environment.

Motivation Quote: "In the language of open communication, your relationships flourish. Each conversation is an opportunity for growth and understanding."

Educating Loved Ones about Bipolar 1

Educating your loved ones about bipolar 1 is instrumental in fostering empathy and dispelling misconceptions. This chapter provides insights into effectively sharing information.

Providing Resources: Share educational resources about bipolar 1 disorder with your loved ones. Books, articles, or reputable websites can offer valuable insights into the nature of the condition and how it may impact your life.

Personalizing the Experience: Share your personal experiences and feelings. Help your loved ones understand how bipolar 1 manifests in your life. Personalizing the experience makes the information more relatable and enhances empathy.

Encouraging Questions: Create an open space for questions and discussions. Encourage your loved ones to ask questions about bipolar 1, fostering an environment where curiosity is met with understanding.

Setting Boundaries and Communicating Needs

Establishing clear boundaries is vital for maintaining healthy relationships. This chapter explores strategies for setting boundaries and effectively communicating your needs.

Understanding Personal Limits: Recognize your own limits and communicate them to your loved ones. Be clear about what you need during different phases of bipolar 1, whether it's additional support, space, or specific forms of communication.

Establishing Emotional Boundaries: During manic or depressive episodes, establish emotional boundaries. Clearly communicate how your loved ones can support you without compromising your mental well-being.

Regular Check-Ins: Schedule regular check-ins to discuss how you're feeling and address any concerns. This proactive approach to communication ensures that potential issues are identified and addressed early on.

Self-Esteem Boost: "In setting boundaries and expressing your needs, you affirm your worthiness of love and understanding. Your voice matters, and your needs are valid."

As you navigate the dynamics of relationships and communication, remember that building strong connections is an ongoing process. In the next chapter, we'll explore strategies for managing bipolar 1 within the context of employment and career, empowering you to find balance and success in the workplace.

Chapter 10: Employment and Career Strategies

Disclosing Bipolar 1 in the Workplace: Pros and Cons

Navigating bipolar 1 in the workplace involves strategic decision-making regarding disclosure. This chapter explores the pros and cons of disclosing your condition at work.

Pros of Disclosure:

- **Accommodations:** Disclosing bipolar 1 may qualify you for workplace accommodations that support your well-being.

- **Reduced Stigma:** Open discussions about mental health contribute to reducing stigma in the workplace.

- **Improved Understanding:** Colleagues and superiors may gain a better understanding of your needs, fostering a supportive environment.

Cons of Disclosure:

- **Stigma and Discrimination:** Despite efforts to reduce stigma, disclosing bipolar 1 may still lead to discrimination or bias.

- **Privacy Concerns:** Sharing personal health information may impact your privacy in the workplace.

- **Misunderstanding:** Colleagues may not fully understand the nature of bipolar 1, leading to misconceptions.

Motivation Quote: "Your decision to disclose is a personal choice. Whether or not you share, your value in the workplace remains unwavering."

Career Planning with Bipolar 1: Finding Balance

Striking a balance in your career is essential for managing bipolar 1 effectively. This chapter explores strategies for career planning that align with your well-being.

Self-Assessment: Conduct a self-assessment to identify your strengths, preferences, and potential triggers. Choose a career path that aligns with your skills and minimizes stressors.

Flexibility and Adaptability: Seek careers that offer flexibility and adaptability. Jobs with variable schedules or remote work options may provide the space needed to manage bipolar 1 effectively.

Building a Supportive Network: Cultivate a supportive professional network. Colleagues, mentors, and supervisors who understand your needs contribute to a positive and inclusive work environment.

Managing Workplace Stress: Tips for Success

Effectively managing workplace stress is crucial for individuals with bipolar 1. This chapter explores practical tips for navigating stress in the professional setting.

Time Management: Prioritize tasks, set realistic deadlines, and break down larger projects into manageable steps. Effective time management reduces stress and enhances productivity.

Communication Skills: Develop strong communication skills to express your needs clearly. Negotiate workload adjustments when necessary and advocate for a work environment that supports your mental health.

Self-Care at Work: Incorporate self-care practices into your work routine. Take short breaks, practice mindfulness, or engage in activities that promote relaxation to manage stress during the workday.

Self-Esteem Boost: "In your career journey, your unique strengths shine. Embrace the path that aligns with your well-being, and remember, your potential is limitless."

As you navigate the professional landscape with bipolar 1, recognize that your career is a significant aspect of your life journey. In the final chapter, we'll explore the overarching theme of resilience and empowerment, providing insights and encouragement for your ongoing journey with bipolar 1.

Chapter 11: Thriving in Times of Stability

Embracing Stability: Setting and Achieving Realistic Goals

Stability in the journey of bipolar 1 is an achievement worthy of celebration. This chapter explores the importance of setting and achieving realistic goals during times of stability.

Goal Setting: Define short-term and long-term goals that align with your aspirations and well-being. Setting realistic and achievable goals provides direction and purpose.

Breaking Down Goals: Divide larger goals into smaller, manageable tasks. This approach not only makes goals more achievable but also allows for a sense of accomplishment at each step.

Adapting to Change: Acknowledge that goals may need adjustment over time. Be flexible in adapting to changing circumstances while maintaining a forward trajectory.

Motivation Quote: "In embracing stability, you become the architect of your future. Each goal achieved is a testament to your resilience."

The Importance of Continued Therapy and Check-Ins

Maintaining stability involves ongoing self-reflection and support. This chapter explores the significance of continued therapy and regular check-ins.

Therapy as a Tool: Even in times of stability, therapy remains a valuable tool. Regular sessions provide a space for reflection, skill-building, and addressing evolving needs.

Check-Ins with Support System: Periodic check-ins with your support system, including friends and family, contribute to maintaining connections. Open communication ensures that your loved ones remain aware of your well-being.

Monitoring Mental Health: Keep a proactive approach to mental health by monitoring your well-being. Recognize any subtle changes in mood or behavior, addressing them promptly with the support of professionals if needed.

Celebrating Milestones: Recognizing Personal Growth

Celebrate the milestones achieved on your journey with bipolar 1. This chapter explores the importance of recognizing and celebrating personal growth.

Acknowledging Progress: Regularly acknowledge the progress you've made in managing bipolar 1. Celebrate the milestones, whether big or small, as markers of personal growth.

Self-Reflection: Engage in self-reflection to appreciate the resilience and strength you've developed. Recognize the coping strategies that have proven effective and identify areas for further growth.

Gratitude Practices: Incorporate gratitude practices into your routine. Expressing gratitude for the positive aspects of your journey fosters a positive mindset and reinforces resilience.

Self-Esteem Boost: "Celebrating your journey is an affirmation of your strength and growth. Each milestone reached is a testament to your unwavering spirit."

As you navigate times of stability, embrace the opportunity for personal growth and self-discovery. Your journey with bipolar 1 is unique, and your resilience is a source of inspiration. In closing, remember that thriving in times of stability is a continuous process of self-nurturing and empowerment.

Chapter 12: Long-Term Strategies and Future Outlook

Navigating Aging with Bipolar 1

As you embark on the long-term journey with bipolar 1, considerations for aging become significant. This chapter explores strategies for navigating aging while managing bipolar 1.

Health Maintenance: Prioritize overall health by maintaining a balanced lifestyle. Regular exercise, a nutritious diet, and sufficient sleep contribute to physical and mental well-being.

Adapting to Changing Needs: Recognize that the management of bipolar 1 may evolve with age. Be open to adjustments in treatment plans and coping strategies that align with changing needs.

Social Connections: Cultivate and maintain social connections. Strong support systems remain essential throughout life, providing emotional support and understanding.

Motivation Quote: "Aging with bipolar 1 is a testament to your resilience. Your journey continues to unfold, filled with opportunities for growth and fulfillment."

Adjusting Treatment Plans Over Time

Long-term management of bipolar 1 requires periodic adjustments to treatment plans. This chapter explores the importance of adapting treatment strategies over time.

Regular Consultations: Schedule regular consultations with your healthcare provider. Periodic assessments ensure that your treatment plan aligns with your current needs and goals.

Medication Reviews: Review medication effectiveness and potential side effects. Adjustments to dosages or exploring new medications may be necessary to optimize stability.

Therapeutic Support: Ongoing therapy remains a valuable component of long-term management. Regular sessions provide a space for addressing evolving challenges and enhancing coping strategies.

Inspiring Others: Becoming a Mental Health Advocate

As you navigate your long-term journey with bipolar 1, consider the impactful role of mental health advocacy. This chapter explores ways to inspire others and become an advocate for mental health awareness.

Sharing Your Story: Consider sharing your experiences with bipolar 1 to inspire others on their journeys. Personal narratives contribute to reducing stigma and fostering a sense of community.

Participating in Advocacy Initiatives: Engage in mental health advocacy initiatives. Whether through local organizations or online platforms, advocacy efforts play a crucial role in promoting awareness and understanding.

Supporting Community: Offer support to individuals within the bipolar 1 community. Your insights and encouragement can make a meaningful difference in someone else's journey.

Self-Esteem Boost: "Becoming an advocate is a powerful affirmation of your strength and resilience. Your journey inspires others to embrace their own paths with courage."

As you embrace the long-term strategies and future outlook, remember that your journey with bipolar 1 is a continuous narrative of strength and growth. Your resilience not only shapes your own path but also inspires others to navigate their unique journeys with hope and determination.

Conclusion: Empowered Living with Bipolar 1

Reflecting on the Journey

As we conclude this comprehensive guide to managing bipolar 1, take a moment to reflect on the remarkable journey you've undertaken. From understanding the nuances of the disorder to implementing practical strategies for stability, your resilience shines through each chapter.

Acknowledging Growth: Celebrate the growth you've experienced on this journey. Each challenge faced and conquered, each coping strategy embraced, has contributed to your strength and resilience.

Embracing Vulnerability: Recognize the power in embracing vulnerability. Your openness to understanding and managing bipolar 1 reflects not only courage but also a commitment to empowered living.

Encouragement for a Fulfilling and Stable Future

Looking ahead, envision a future marked by fulfillment and stability. Your commitment to well-being and the strategies you've embraced position you for continued success in managing bipolar 1.

Setting Intentions: Set intentions for your future, considering both personal and professional aspirations. Goal-setting provides a roadmap for the fulfilling life you envision.

Cultivating Connections: Nurture your support system and continue building connections. Your relationships are invaluable pillars of strength, providing understanding and encouragement.

Embracing Stability: Embrace the stability you've worked hard to achieve. Your journey is an ongoing process, and by continuing to implement the strategies learned, you pave the way for a more stable and fulfilling life.

Resources for Ongoing Support

Empowered living involves ongoing support and resources. As you move forward, remember that assistance is readily available, and seeking support is a sign of strength.

Therapeutic Continuity: Maintain regular therapy sessions to ensure ongoing support and guidance. Your therapist is a valuable partner in your journey.

Community Engagement: Stay connected with the bipolar 1 community. Online forums, support groups, and advocacy initiatives provide a sense of belonging and shared understanding.

Continued Education: Stay informed about the latest developments in bipolar 1 management. Continued education empowers you with knowledge and strengthens your ability to navigate the complexities of the disorder.

Self-Esteem Boost: "In embracing your journey with bipolar 1, you affirm your capacity for growth and resilience. Your path is unique, and your potential is boundless."

As you step into the future, carry with you the wisdom gained from this guide, the strength forged in overcoming challenges, and the hope for a fulfilling and stable life. You are not alone, and your journey is a testament to the resilience within. Here's to empowered living with bipolar 1 and the endless possibilities that await you.

Appendix: Additional Resources and Worksheets

Recommended Reading List

Explore the following books for further insights and guidance on bipolar 1 disorder:

1. **"An Unquiet Mind" by Kay Redfield Jamison:** A poignant memoir by a clinical psychologist with bipolar disorder, offering a personal and professional perspective.

2. **"The Bipolar Disorder Survival Guide" by David J. Miklowitz:** A comprehensive guide covering practical strategies for managing bipolar disorder and fostering stability.

3. **"Madness: A Bipolar Life" by Marya Hornbacher:** A raw and honest memoir that provides a vivid account of living with bipolar disorder.

4. **"Bipolar Happens! 35 Tips and Tricks to Manage Bipolar Disorder" by Julie A. Fast:** A practical guide offering tips and strategies for navigating the challenges of bipolar disorder.

5. **"Loving Someone with Bipolar Disorder" by Julie A. Fast and John D. Preston:** A guide for friends and family, providing insights into supporting loved ones with bipolar disorder.

Worksheets for Self-Reflection and Planning

1. **Goal-Setting Worksheet:**

   - Define short-term and long-term goals related to your well-being.

   - Break down goals into actionable steps.

   - Set realistic deadlines and track progress.

2. **Mood Journal:**

   - Maintain a daily journal to track mood fluctuations.

   - Record factors influencing mood changes.

   - Identify patterns and potential triggers.

3. **Self-Care Planner:**

   - List self-care activities that promote well-being.

   - Schedule regular self-care practices.

   - Prioritize self-care during challenging times.

4. **Support System Inventory:**

   - Identify individuals in your support system.

   - Note their roles and how they can offer support.

   - Regularly assess and update your support network.

Directory of Mental Health Organizations and Support Groups

1. **National Alliance on Mental Illness (NAMI):**

   - Website: www.nami.org

   - NAMI provides resources, support, and advocacy for individuals and families affected by mental health conditions.

2. **Depression and Bipolar Support Alliance (DBSA):**

   - Website: www.dbsalliance.org

- DBSA offers peer-led support groups and resources for individuals living with mood disorders.

3. **Mental Health America (MHA):**

   - Website: www.mhanational.org

   - MHA advocates for mental health awareness, provides resources, and offers screening tools.

4. **International Bipolar Foundation (IBPF):**

   - Website: www.ibpf.org

   - IBPF focuses on education, support, and advocacy for individuals affected by bipolar disorder.

5. **PsychCentral Bipolar Disorder Forum:**

   - Forum: Bipolar Disorder Forum

   - An online community where individuals can share experiences, seek advice, and connect with others.

Explore these resources to enhance your understanding, access support, and connect with a broader community. Remember, seeking help is a proactive step toward empowered living with bipolar 1.

Dear Reader,

Thank you for embarking on the journey of "Navigating Bipolar 1: A Comprehensive Guide to Managing Your Symptoms." Your commitment to understanding and improving your life is commendable. May the insights gained empower you to navigate challenges with resilience, celebrate victories, and thrive in your unique journey. Remember, you're not alone, and your dedication to growth is a testament to your strength. Here's to a life filled with stability, fulfillment, and the unwavering belief in your potential.

With gratitude,

Sean Williams